women's poetry anthology

EMILY DICKINSON   EMMA LAZARUS

LADY GREGORY

ELIZABETH BARRETT BROWNING

THE WHORE OF QUALITY   SAPPHO

GERTRUDE STEIN   WHITNEE COY

CASEY LAWRENCE   LINDA ROSEWOOD

HOLLY PAYNE-STRANGE   ALICE DUER MILLER

VICTORIA MINEVA   ALEXANDRIA TANNENBAUM

BAILEY GREY   JUDITH SKILLMAN

TAMARA HOLMAN   FIONA RICHARDSON

BARBARA ANN MEIER HOLTZ

ELLEN S. ROMANO   PULKITA ANAND

SUZANNE MORRIS   ELSA GIDLOW

JUDY CLARENCE   TARA SCHAUBERT

EDITED BY

LANCELOT SCHAUBERT

Schaubert, Lancelot

WOMEN'S POETRY ANTHOLOGY / Lancelot Schaubert

ISBN: 978-1-949547-22-1

POETRY / WOMEN AUTHORS

SOCIAL SCIENCE / ABORTION AND BIRTH CONTROL

POETRY / GENERAL / ASIAN

POETRY / SUBJECTS AND THEMES / LOVE & EROTICA

Printed in the United States of America

Lemniscate Of Bernoulli Props - Right Hand Loop Of Lemniscate —for image between chapters.

contents

introduction

LANCELOT SCHAUBERT, EDITOR

I am the least qualified person to write this introduction, let alone edit this volume, which explains how desperately we need more books like this one. I say "least" because I am neither a woman, nor a lauded poetry editor. So who do I think I am, publishing something like this?

The last one left in a room on fire, I guess.

It's not that similar things haven't been tried, that tangentially *related* volumes haven't existed, but the existence of this one is quite simple, really. It's honestly the weirdest, most unconventional way I've ever decided to make a book. I have an app named Publisher Rocket that helps me select categories and keywords for my books, those I edit or write. In researching another book, the keyword Women's Poetry Anthology came across my desk. I clicked on it almost at random to see the competition. It was basically zero. I did some digging and other than certain old anthologies, it seemed to me that nothing new was being made. I dug a little deeper in the Submission Grinder and Duotrope and Submittable submission pages and found, again, nothing. It's rather funny to me. People say all of the time that poetry doesn't sell (I think the existence of Kendrick Lamar and advertising jingles says otherwise, but table that for the moment). It was through marketing research that I got the idea for this poetry anthology.

Be the change and all that, I guess.

I was shocked, but it seemed to me the best course of action was to open up for submissions once more, this time for an anthology of new women writers to be published alongside some of my favorite public domain poems by women.

Again, I'm not the greatest poetry judge. Nor am I a woman.

I was just looking around the room, waiting for someone to point out the fire that had kindled in the corner. Someone to mention it, mention the smoke. Someone to clear the room or even scream or just... you know... gesture vaguely in that direction. Since no one seemed to be picking up the extinguisher in the middle of the floor, I did.

I'm grateful to these women for trusting me with their words.

But I'm far more grateful for the words themselves. They moved me. They'll move you too.

ELIZABETH BARRETT BROWNING

And wilt thou have me fashion into speech
The love I bear thee, finding words enough,
And hold the torch out, while the winds are rough,
Between our faces, to cast light on each?—
I drop it at thy feet. I cannot teach
My hand to hold my spirits so far off
From myself—me—that I should bring thee proof
In words, of love hid in me out of reach.
Nay, let the silence of my womanhood
Commend my woman-love to thy belief,—
Seeing that I stand unwon, however wooed,
And rend the garment of my life, in brief,
By a most dauntless, voiceless fortitude,
Lest one touch of this heart convey its grief.

The night I was dying
my eyes were swollen shut as
the hospital bed's sheets
were changed repeatedly
from being soaked
in my urine & vomit.

The night I was dying
my nurse cradled my body
& held me, rocking me
in her chest as I cupped
my pregnant belly.

I didn't die that night.

Although white lab coats
scampered around my limp
frame like field mice.
Low voices hummed as if it were a secret
my body was shutting down.
Turning off the lights in each room
one at a time.

A month & a half later

in the NICU while holding my 3.5-pound
baby, a woman with a rusted-clamp clipboard
nattered about the weather, specifically the wind &
    gloom
as I had spent 4 hours in a room with no windows
holding the shell that was my baby.
Finally, she fumbled about what she was there
    to ask:
How was I processing my near-death
experience & traumatic birth?

I didn't know.
Just like I didn't know how many
ounces I had pumped alone, & baby-less
being told to look at a photo of my daughter
in an incubator to try to squeeze
out more drops of milk.
I didn't know the last time I had brushed
my teeth or if my stitches had dissolved.
I didn't know when my baby would
or could ever breathe on her own.

I didn't know how I had spent days
in sterile hospital sheets & was expected to
    go home
without my baby & act as if the story were
    the same
because we had both lived.

How do I explain, all I did was spin
around the idea that the only thing I had ever
    grown
had stopped moving the day I was dying?

hostel

CASEY LAWRENCE

Tumbling bedward
on the precipice of sleep,
her hair catches the light
like a halo of stars

and I, like a thief,
steal another glance
before closing the door
between our rooms

as i stroll

HOLLY PAYNE-STRANGE

I'm not a fool you know,
I know what is -probably- coming next.
But I also know what I would write,
If this were a fairytale, or some romantic epic.
I would set it in the regency period, of course.
So I could have flowing silk skirts,
Glittering gold embroidery in English gardens,
And you, somehow both somber and resplendent
In a top hat and tails. Lace at your neck that I'd
    have to undo...

Forgive me a moment, I am distracted...

Ah, but I would also want the heroine
Me
To go down in a blaze of glory
Embrace the adventure,
Set sail, searching for new worlds,
After she had kindly and artfully
Told the old one to fuck off.
Never once giving up, never wavering from her
Heart's desire.

Even in the darkest of times.

And so
That is exactly what I plan to do.
I would ask for luck
But I don't need it.
I know what I'm doing.

the grief of a girl's heart

TRANSLATED FROM THE IRISH BY
LADY GREGORY

O DONALL OG, if you go across the sea, bring myself with you and do not forget it; and you will have a sweetheart for fair days and market days, and the daughter of the King of Greece beside you at night. It is late last night the dog was speaking of you; the snipe was speaking of you in her deep marsh. It is you are the lonely bird through the woods; and that you may be without a mate until you find me.

You promised me, and you said a lie to me, that you would be before me where the sheep are flocked; I gave a whistle and three hundred cries to you, and I found nothing there but a bleating lamb.

You promised me a thing that was hard for you, a ship of gold under a silver mast; twelve towns with a market in all of them, and a fine white court by the side of the sea.

You promised me a thing that is not possible, that you would give me gloves of the skin of a fish; that you would give me shoes of the skin of a bird, and a suit of the dearest silk in Ireland.

O Donall og, it is I would be better to you than a high, proud, spendthrift lady: I would milk the cow; I would bring help to you; and if you were hard pressed, I would strike a blow for you.

O, ochone, and it's not with hunger or with wanting

food, or drink, or sleep, that I am grow- ing thin, and my life is shortened; but it is the love of a young man has withered me away.

It is early in the morning that I saw him coming, going along the road on the back of a horse; he did not come to me; he made nothing of me; and it is on my way home that I cried my fill.

When I go by myself to the Well of Loneliness, I sit down and I go through my trouble; when I see the world and do not see my boy, he that has an amber shade in his hair.

It was on that Sunday I gave my love to you; the Sunday that is last before Easter Sunday. And myself on my knees reading the Passion; and my two eyes giving love to you for ever.

O, aya! my mother, give myself to him; and give him all that you have in the world; get out yourself to ask for alms, and do not come back and forward looking for me.

My mother said to me not to be talking with you to-day, or to-morrow, or on the Sunday; it was a bad time she took for telling me that; it was shutting the door after the house was robbed.

My heart is as black as the blackness of the sloe, or as the black coal that is on the smith's forge; or as the sole of a shoe left in white halls; it was you put that darkness over my life.

You have taken the east from me; you have taken the west from me; you have taken what is before me and what is behind me; you have taken the moon, you have taken the sun from me; and my fear is great that you have taken God from me!

ode to anactoria

SAPPHO

TRANSLATED BY H. DE VERE
STACPOOLE

Peer of Gods to me is the man thy presence
Crowns with joy; who hears, as he sits beside thee,
Accents sweet of thy lips the silence breaking,
With lovely laughter;

Tones that make the heart in my bosom flutter,
For if I, the space of a moment even,
Near to thee come, any word I would utter
Instantly fails me;

Vain my stricken tongue would a whisper fashion,
Subtly under my skin runs fire ecstatic;
Straightway mists surge dim to my eyes and
    leave them
Reft of their vision;

Echoes ring in my ears; a trembling seizes
All my body bathed in soft perspiration;
Pale as grass I grow in my passion's madness,
Like one insensate;

But must I dare all, since to me unworthy,
Bliss thy beauty brings that a god might envy;
Never yet was fervid woman a fairer

Image of Kypris.

Ah! undying Daughter of God, befriend me!
Calm my blood that thrills with impending
　　transport;
Feed my lips the murmur of words to stir her
Bosom to pity;

Overcome with kisses her faintest protest,
Melt her mood to mine with amorous touches,
Till her low assent and her sigh's abandon
Lure me to rapture.

demeter's head

HOLLY PAYNE-STRANGE

Everyday I talk to my garden.
To the white pot, now cracked and chipped,
Dirt tumbling through the bottom,
And purple flowers cascading out the top.
A halo of purple flowers,
Cascading around the cheeks
Of my Goddess.

I tell her what I want,
And what I'm afraid of,
Spilling the details of my day,
Like birdseed, hoping to attract a little magic.
Inviting Hermes in too, if he wants,
Saying hi to Hestia.

And I feel such peace,
As if for a moment I have been allowed to land,
Rest a white,
Checking my plumage, seeing what feathers I
     have lost
And gained
Throughout the day.

The breeze rustles the leaves,
Fresh and cool.
The clouds part, bright sunlight now on my face
And I know
The birdseed worked.

many men to any woman

ALICE DUER MILLER

If you have beauty, charm, refinement, tact,
If you can prove that should I set you free,
You would not contemplate the smallest act
That might annoy or interfere with me.
If you can show that women will abide
By the best standards of their womanhood—
(And I must be the person to decide
What in a woman is the highest good);
If you display efficiency supreme
In philanthropic work devoid of pay;
If you can show a clearly thought-out scheme
For bringing the millennium in a day:
Why, then, dear lady, at some time remote,
I might consider giving you the vote.

the third road

FIONA RICHARDSON

A mile, or maybe two, outside St. Ives,
Walking along the clifftop's winding path
Near sunset, in the day's long aftermath,
The rusty light over the riffling waves,
I see three or four dragons, peacefully
Dipping their giant heads as if to drink.
Or are they rocks? They alter, blink by blink,
And is that lapping dragons or the sea?
The twilight blooms an otherworldly blue
And this sublunar world grows thrawn and frail;
That other world draws closer to a veil
So delicate some stars are showing through.
And I walk onward, seeking out the way,
The path that winds about the fernie brae.

sand steps

VICTORIA MINEVA

I drove to the beach,
Meeting the sand stories
Those waves washed away
Like my own memories
One step on the left, the other on the right
Sadness walked into my mind
I wonder again how I survived
The pain inside and the sorrow
He made me a whole
Now, nothing at all
Tossing my feeling
Under the dome
Stepping in water
I saw jellyfish
I stumbled on the stone
Creating plain wish
Only to be loved
Sand smiled at me
My steps didn't exist
They were covered

*picturing my
mother as a
teenager*

ALEXANDRIA TANNENBAUM

growing Up

with no money to travel,
sisters met their father on business trips
door full of movie stubs,
playing kickball in the street
spending the evenings at the beach
with dinner in a tight picnic basket
with no money to travel,
sisters met their fathers less and less
mom stayed up late
listening to the hum of piano keys
and the scrape of a glass
as the condensation soaked through
with no money to travel,
sisters sat watching years pass like cars in the
        night
segmented bathing suit bikini
in hotel pools sun against the splash
skin warming and collecting sun spots

my mother's mother

died the year after i was born

oh, to be a new mother
without your mother
to be a mother and outlive your daughter
they found her on the bathroom floor
after the first aneurysm,
grandmother moved in
stared at the glow of the tv
late at night with her grandchildren
soft skinned hand cradling salty popcorn
they said their final goodbyes
the slow dim
like a cigarette left in the bowl
someone left the window open
and the slight breeze
scattered gray ash
all across the kitchen table

looking back,

the hardest part of growing up
is counting back the years that have gone
easy like filing away another receipt or bill paid
and full the way it feels
like standing abruptly at the dinner table
chair pushed back up against the wall
the hardest part of growing up
is driving home for the last time
wishing the holidays would pass quicker
as they become unbearable longing and loss
the hardest part of growing up
is when you read your mother's handwriting
the letters she sent you at camp
the recipes with splattered tomato sauce and oil
    stains
the post-it note she left as a last minute reminder
and know that someday
this will be all the words she will ever have to give

rutting season

JUDY CLARENCE

Three deer in the driveway,
one an unafraid buck,
antlers thick as my arms,
as wide as I can make them spread.
He stares. I avert my eyes.
His are brown as chocolate kisses.
He stands between me
and the does. Doesn't budge.
Looking at the ground, the cracked
gravel grooves spreading toward
the edge, I circle sideways,
not to be a threat. He stares.
He does not move. I softly say,
"It's OK. I'm just walking past."
He puffs and moves aside. We both
know war, conflict, hot angry breaths
are not antidotes to fear.

it started at a slow pace.

VICTORIA MINEVA

Between The Raven and Valery Black
There was a chemistry in their pack
But he left her for better omega wolf-like
She continued forward, riding the hollow's bike
When left alone, Valery was sad
It took her time to go back
To her original soul face
It started at a slow pace

in "all creatures
great and small"...

SUZANNE MORRIS

Helen and James got married
in Episode 1 of Season 3

the bride radiant in her
white wedding gown,

a bouquet of pink peonies
clasped in her trembling hands

the groom scrambling into his
wedding suit

en route to the church
in Siegfried's car,

after a full morning of
tuberculin-testing cows.

What a beguiling couple
we've always agreed

sitting together
in front of our TV.

Watched rapt through
Seasons 1 and 2

as romance bloomed
like mountain pansy
on the Yorkshire Dales

with Siegfried and Tristan,
Mrs. Hall and Jess the good dog

carrying on at Skeldale House.

Alas, I attended the wedding alone
as you fell asleep in your chair

too exhausted from struggling
to rouse yourself, to care.

When the couple
recited the age-old vows

I knew they were in the
wrong order.

We do not love each other
in sickness and in health:

first comes youth and vitality,
then, crushing illness

...till death do us part...

as it had done
to you and me

before Episode 2 of Season 3.

the wife

EMILY DICKINSON

She rose to his requirement, dropped
The playthings of her life
To take the honorable work
Of woman and of wife.

If aught she missed in her new day
Of amplitude, or awe,
Or first prospective, or the gold
In using wore away,

It lay unmentioned, as the sea
Develops pearl and weed,
But only to himself is known
The fathoms they abide.

tule lake

BARBARA ANN MEIER HOLTZ

The hare quivers amongst the bunchgrass,
while the western rattler uncoils in baking
    sunlight,
singing with the locust, clicking
in the heated scent of purple medicine sage.
The Myotis bats stay asleep in the coolness
of the underground caves of broken lava tubes.

It brings to mind, a remembering
of the passage of boats on a lake
rising and falling in rifts of time,
watching the ancients chiseling glyphs
on a wall of tuff.
An island sacred to the departed dwellers,
giving significance, long forgotten,
except by the Modoc elders.

The hare and the rattler meet in the shade
of a juniper bush, where the sun boiled needles
    rest,
the locust embraced by the sticky tongue of the
    western skink,
and the Myotis bats succumb to white nose
    syndrome.

Captain Jack is dead and the Modoc tribe scattered,
leaving only tourists at the dusty fence on a dried
up lake.

wonder

TARA SCHAUBERT

Crash
Bang
Boom
It's a little
Boy's
Room

playground diptych

AFTER JENNY XIE

ALEXANDRIA TANNENBAUM

I.

The reds here bleed. Swings awash in yellow and
    blue buckles. Freckled with sun, and failing
    paint, they stronghold what's left of the day.

We are fortunate to be here to have this time,
    which doesn't seem to be running out.

The splendor finds ways to settle in the sit down.
    The run through. The call of children.

The teacher, perspiration beading on her forehead,
    thinks of ways to stop the echo. The kids
    starting fires in her room, the seep of doubt as
    she turns her back to the crowd. Chalk dust
    whirls in the light from the window.

Yes, there are tunnels, and no, the sun doesn't
    reach inside where plastic holds onto plastic.
    Do you hide in here often?

Weeping willows bend thin branches toward the

ground. Swaying in the afternoon of things.
There is a chain fence here too. Did you see it?

The bottom of the slide is cracked. Jagged shards of
blue push up into the afternoon sky. As kids
slide down, they grimace and hold tight to
their legs. No one ever tells the supervisor. Not
here.

II.

Even when we age out of play, we are still mirrored
by the time we grow old. We need to decide
how to end this chapter.

Yes, you could tell someone, but will they always
remember the way your voice quivered?

Yes, you could keep it to yourself, but will you ever
forgive the way you carried it through the
years?

Once, I tried to jump it when time would not leave
me alone. Once, we hid behind the trunks of
trees thinking we could hide from the day. And
we never could. Or will.

Even with yearly goodbyes, we never leave that
fence, the dust from the baseball diamond, the
empty bench when everyone else was invited
to play. The way that childhood seems like an
endless winter night.

And in each classroom, kids in desks, trying to ig-
nore the chorus of what was said about them,

the shadows of all the ways they try to disappear.

enchanted strand

FOR MY FRIEND WHO IS FAR
AWAY AND WE ARE GETTING
OLDER.

LINDA ROSEWOOD

Yet I am fain to share with others the subtle enchantment of the place, the strangeness of it. Perhaps through strength of such a wish it may chance that someone lingering hereafter on the strand at Inch, someone even who will never venture there, may touch hearts with me—myself long dead.

—Ella Young

Summoned here by a long dead witch,
Lingering on the breezy strand at Inch,
I find myself missing my friend.

So I make a labyrinth in the sand with the heel of
    my boot.
Curve and curve, this sigil invokes her
From her floured kitchen and buttery bed,
Wearing my earrings.
Across the Atlantic to this wild dune
Over-sung by skylarks.

I loved her first in a labyrinth and we never left it.
We drew labyrinths in meadows,
Messing with a magic I didn't understand.
Meeting and parting we passed, fingertips
     touching,
Sharing lifetimes of love, all wreckage and joy.

We thinned apples. We bought her first ipad.
Her cats commented querulously.
I drank her cider and chewed her bread.
We took the ferry to Ptown and walked Mary's
     dunes.

That one time when I thought we'd be neighbors.
But here's a curve, and I go in a different direction.
At sixty, I've learned labyrinths are not whimsy.
They are the longest thing we'll know.

Today at Inch, I tread this fresh labyrinth,
Curve and curve.
At the center I call her name and the witch appears
Touching hearts with us. Here you're both young.

Grass grew tall in the meadow above the orchard.
She bought a new ipad.
She shared around that pressing of Kingston Black
     cider.
Her cats lived on in memory.
Mary Oliver died.

Driven sand buries the labyrinth as soon as I
     leave it.
I race Ella's wavelets.
Skylarks praise the sun higher and higher.
I understand the form of this long enchantment:
Curve and curve.
Meeting and parting, never lost.

bride

SAPPHO

TRANSLATED BY H. DE VERE
STACPOOLE

Bride, that goest to the bridal chamber
In the dove-drawn car of Aphrodite,
By a band of dimpled
Loves surrounded;

Bride, of maidens all the fairest image
Mitylene treasures of the Goddess,
Rosy-ankled Graces
Are thy playmates;

Bride, O fair and lovely, thy companions
Are the gracious hours that onward passing
For thy gladsome footsteps
Scatter garlands.

Bride, that blushing like the sweetest apple
On the very branch's end, so strangely
Overlooked, ungathered
By the gleaners;

Bride, that like the apple that was never
Overlooked but out of reach so plainly,
Only one thy rarest
Fruit may gather;

Bride, that into womanhood has ripened
For the harvest of the bridegroom only,
He alone shall taste thy
Hoarded sweetness.

BAILEY GREY

Growing up in the pure warmth of a spotlight
Makes it that much more freezing once you
Move away.

Plain white audition waiting- rooms,
Musical posters from every decade
hanging from the walls.
Sweaty nervous children,
Girls with glimmering pink bows in their hair.
I was never the same as them, you see.
The colour I wore was olive green —
To match my eyes.
You can imagine why my developing brain felt
Out of place.

Not all people were kind.
There is a level of kindness that
should
be required when casting a child in a role.
I began to think the way men spoke to me
Was just to give direction.

Weigh-ins. Height measurements.
Keep track of the growth.

'When you get too tall,
We'll have to fire you.
Everything you put into this will cease to exist
     because
Sweetie, You're growing!'

And I was growing.
Too quickly.
I learned things way too soon,
Shooting myself in the foot with other kids my age.
The ones of us who weren't being called
Sweetie
by big time Theatre Executives.

Did they really want to be my friends?
Or were they living vicariously?
At least I gave them a false life to live.

"Get your foot in the door before you're 18"
What door?
You mean the same one that shuts itself to
     me now?
Just because I am no longer
Sweet,
Innocent,
Impressionable?

I'm still here.
I still want it.
I long to stand in the blazing heat of a stage
To step into a character,
Discover what makes them
Tick.

All the years I spent in audition rooms,
On stages across the country,
Creating worlds with
The best of the best.
I would not trade you for a thing,

I just expected more kindness
after the fact.
Always more kindness.

I know what to expect now.
Two Arts degrees and
Maybe an audition once every month. Or two...
    months.

They all tried to warn me,
I'd be working a job I hate "in the meantime."
I never believed them.
I knew my worth.
But it's not my worth that's keeping me from being
    in the room.
It's the way the door opens.
My foot is only so big.
All I need is a bigger
push
from the inside.

the privileged man

JUDITH SKILLMAN

Outside our rooms, cold
shivers its way in
through cracks in a ruse.

Ours a conditional warmth
dependent upon rituals of chivalry.
Doors open and close soundlessly

for his late arrival,
woman on his arm for ornament.
Testament to hours of colors

brushed and painted
to hold a youngish face in place.
He discourses with men of his ilk,

scientists and gormandizers for whom
custodians create order at dawn.
Night is a book with no writing.

*intertwined at
the root*

WHITNEE COY

They never tell you
that for the first six months of life
your baby has no understanding
that their little-limbed body
is no longer connected,
intertwined at the root
with yours.

They never mention to you
that your baby can't comprehend
that you don't feel their hunger,
as they squeal, lungs opening from the inside out.
Convinced they will never eat again & you
save them each time. They don't know
their whelps of fear with quivering bottom lips
& arms flinging out as you push
their toes into their onesie's feet
isn't as frightening to you.
That you understand they aren't disappearing.
Or that the heartbeat of yours
they hear, echoing in a silent vessel of their body
isn't their own anymore.
You can exist without one another.

How could you possibly expect her,
as delicate as a new web-spotted
with rain after a summer storm,
to know so much
of this deep, wide, dark world?

bookmarks

CASEY LAWRENCE

It was a Tuesday morning,
grey and drizzling,
like wet newspaper ink
running into the gutters
from all the uncollected papers
with their want ads
uncircled by red pen.

It was a Tuesday morning
that the neighbors found him
in the closed garage,
reclined in his janky Buick
with a newspaper held loosely
in ashen, paperthin hands
with a thumb between two pages
of the cartoon section.

It was a Tuesday afternoon
when they called his daughter
and she took a flight out
from Arizona
to see the toe-tag for herself
and leaf through pamphlets,
angry at the binder

with its colored tabs
marking the payment plans
and arrangement packages
with too-cheerful bookmarks
of red and blue and yellow.

It had been a Tuesday morning
when he'd been called by his boss
and got the news of the layoff,
with three years left
before retirement.

It had been a Tuesday morning
when the last payslip cleared
and he had already gone door-to-door
with printed résumés
and applications in a binder
with color-coded tabs.

It had been a Tuesday morning
when the power was shut off
for nonpayment
and the red-stamped envelope
was useless except to mark
the back of the Yellowpages
where he'd finished calling
every business in the phonebook
before the line went dead.

It was a Tuesday night
when his daughter,
whose name was Iris,
like the flower,
found the final notices
and the unpaid bills
and the polite rejections
and the newspaper ads
organized alphabetically
in her high school math binder,

with engineer precision
except for the creased corners
bookmarking unanswered calls.

It wasn't until the next Friday
when she had the power back on
in his creaky old Bungalow
and the computer booted up
to a bookmarked webpage
(visited sixty-three times)
with the number
for the suicide hotline
that she finally heard
all the cries for help
pressed between the pages
of the newspaper
with the corners
bent.

gen x and
archaeological
suffrage

TAMARA HOLMAN

"Is it better?" the Gen Z tech asked, shouting to
be heard above the clamber of the conference
mixer. I want to tell them yes, that the toil of
those who came before us made it better. The
moil of the Boomer women who wallowed in
the pits, not unlike the welter of academics in
that room, meant that we never contend with
the crushing defeat of

being ignored because of
something as inconsequential
as what genitals we possess.

But those who endeavored before me put up
with sexist slurs from the pit boss and were
afraid to take a shower alone. While I haven't
felt that fear; I had an experience where my
professor ogled me from head to toe while
saying:

"Yeah, I've heard you are good."

I want to say we have overcome, but today I
was ignored in the taxicab that I invited my

academic elders to ride in. They were deep in conversation in the back seat about my session topic. But then, the Indigenous woman cab driver said:

"Hey, Mr. Know-it-all, listen to her."

Speak up.

FIONA RICHARDSON

In the summer sky, screaming swifts
Power through the air like Red Arrows.
Formation flying over chimneypots,
Crowding the air with their wings' crescents,
One aviator looping into an Immelmann turn,
Another barrel-rolling in aerial joy.

We see them, and feel too that giddy joy,
Our hearts leaping and looping with the swifts.
We welcome them in Spring, as they return
From their long home in Africa, their skeins and
    arrows
Precise under the sun or the moon's crescent,
Over roofs with cracked slates and Victorian chim-
    neypots.

Pelagic bird, from wide oceans to chimneypots,
Nesting in soot and dust, still you bring joy.
Under the eaves your nest's fragile crescent
Your only rest in a life winged and swift
As thought, as lightning, as a well-fletched arrow.
Circling the globe for turn on turn on turn.

The topographical flight of their return,

From African rondavels to Albion's chimneypots,
Over seas, over barren sands, they aim their
     arrows;
Flying without rest, their only joy
Is the journey, the pilgrimage, the swift
Passage to suburban streets and tidy crescents.

Air is their element: their whirling crescent
Shapes in the evening sky as they soar and turn,
Battening on insects, greedily gobbling the swift
High fliers, dodging among the chimneypots,
Spiralling up the thermals in sheer joy,
Needling between the sunbeams and the rain's
     arrows

Back to their swiftlets. These little arrows
Packed tight in the quiver; their mouths' crescents
Gaping for bugs – birds growing into joy,
Fattening, fledging, practising their turn,
Soon balancing on wires and chimneypots,
Readying themselves for that giddy road and swift,

Flying into joy, leaving the chimneypots,
Turning their wheeling crescents into arrows,
Screaming they turn towards the south – the
     swifts.

*this year's hot
shit award
goes to...*

LAUREN SCHAUBERT

I thought I'd give an acceptance speech one day
Thought it would be for some sort of cool award—
I'm hot shit, don'tcha know?
Dad said: "Play stupid games, win stupid prizes."
So now I'm giving an
Acceptance speech
In a church basement: to a group
Of alcoholics who are not so different from me.

ELSA GIDLOW

I have robbed the garrulous streets,
Thieved a fair girl from their blight,
I have stolen her for a sacrifice
That I shall make to this mysteried night.
I have brought her, laughing,
To my quietly sinister garden.
For what will be done there
I ask no man's pardon.
I brush the rouge from her cheeks,
Clean the black kohl from the rims
Of her eyes; loose her hair;
Uncover the glimmering, shy limbs.
I break wild roses, scatter them over her.
The thorns between us sting like love's pain.
Her flesh, bitter and salt to my tongue,
I taste with endless kisses and taste again.
At dawn I leave her
Asleep in my wakening garden.
(For what was done there
I ask no man's pardon.)

rules (advice) for my daughter in time of war

JUDY CLARENCE

Don't look at it. Don't scroll
and click on views of wounds
and flight and huddling in the dark,
in ruins. Read about it all you want;
don't watch. The pictures that form
behind your eyes will be terrible
enough.

Go out into the green earth.
Focus your attention on one bright
leaf. See how it dazzles
where the sun streams down.
Its neighbors are falling, all
around, but that leaf clings tightly
to the branch, and keeps on
singing.

Be that leaf.

celandine
dandelion

FOR HELEN ON HER SEVENTIETH
BIRTHDAY

LINDA ROSEWOOD

Dune
Far west from home
A girl befriends a pyramidal orchid.
She lifts her face in meadowsweet breezes.
Harebells frolic and thin dune grasses draw circles
    in the sand.
She leaves a whisper on a cat's ear.
Her true name.

Bog
In a cottage above the fen—the old ocean's
    finger—
A young mother cooks bread on a turf range
Setting the heat by the palm of her hand.
She feeds her sons and husband,
Imaging a woman, exactly the right temperature.

On fine days she rides her bicycle west
Down narrow roads toward the bog
Where a bastle house defends gorse against all
    enemies.
That proud hall, now roofless, paved with sheep
    shit.
The cellar full of nettles.

Their domination never lasts.

She nearly finds what she came for,
Where flowers bloom for no man's market.
Mostly heather speaking the women's purple
    language.
Once she found a bug-eating sundew.
You adapt when you grow without nourishment.

Wall
Cabbages Cabbages Cabbages.
A long time ago she and her husband
Piled cabbages and carrots along their wall.
She sat for a photo, too tired to notice
Stone-loving periwinkle, teasel, pennywort.

Last spring, she remembered the dry-stone charm
Under smothering vines.
A neighbor warned, don't mess with the ivy,
You could bring the wall down.
She grabbed her sharpest secateurs.
The neighbor didn't realize.
Years ago she'd shifted stones into poems and
Never ate cabbage again.

Wood
"Twayblade." She introduces me to a weed.
Now I see the delicate orchid.
"Primrose."
"Dog Violet."
"Harts Tongue Fern."
"Stitchwort."
Under august beeches she teaches me their names.
I learn to say wood sorrel, never shamrock.
"Celandine dandelion" she says, delighting in the
    melody of two flowers together.

the long marriage prayer

JUDITH SKILLMAN

The lichen and the lichen's kin.
Rabbits black and black and white

sun themselves on winter days.
The dirt road leads to a tenement

where a man and a woman live
to peel back the skin of one

another until inside the core
a self's cut loose to fester and burn.

Do onion tears sting? The lichen
gray on green, the evening lengthening.

Am I in possession of anger
or has it turned, made

an incubus of sensuality
and silence. I wish for a crust

of armor, for stars on snow. I want
to hear the tinkle of snow melt

and know that you left first,
before my soul lost its sensibility.

EMILY DICKINSON

Doubt me, my dim companion!
Why, God would be content
With but a fraction of the love
Poured thee without a stint.
The whole of me, forever,
What more the woman can, —
Say quick, that I may dower thee
With last delight I own!

It cannot be my spirit,
For that was thine before;
I ceded all of dust I knew, —
What opulence the more
Had I, a humble maiden,
Whose farthest of degree
Was that she might,
Some distant heaven,
Dwell timidly with thee!

xviii

I never gave a lock of hair away
To a man, Dearest, except this to thee,
Which now upon my fingers thoughtfully
I ring out to the full brown length and say
"Take it." My day of youth went yesterday;
My hair no longer bounds to my foot's glee,
Nor plant I it from rose- or myrtle-tree,
As girls do, any more: it only may
Now shade on two pale cheeks the mark of tears,
Taught drooping from the head that hangs aside
Through sorrow's trick. I thought the funeral-
    shears
Would take this first, but Love is justified,—
Take it thou,—finding pure, from all those years,
The kiss my mother left here when she died.

a substance in a cushion

GERTRUDE STEIN

THE CHANGE of color is likely and a difference a very little difference is prepared. Sugar is not a vegetable.

Callous is something that hardening leaves behind what will be soft if there is a genuine interest in there being present as many girls as men. Does this change. It shows that dirt is clean when there is a volume.

A cushion has that cover. Supposing you do not like to change, supposing it is very clean that there is no change in appearance, supposing that there is regularity and a costume is that any the worse than an oyster and an exchange. Come to season that is there any extreme use in feather and cotton. Is there not much more joy in a table and more chairs and very likely roundness and a place to put them.

FIONA RICHARDSON

Vulpecula is a minor constellation in the summer sky. The name is usually translated as Little Fox, but the Latin noun is feminine, so she's not a little fox but a little vixen. This is a poem about her.

Little vixen nosing among the nettles,
Snuffling through long grass and dandelions.
Crunching up beetles, slurping snails,
Dancing with gnats and butterflies – a reel, a jig –
To the music of the summer breeze,
Busily digging in the peaty earth.
What worms and diamonds
Will she bring out into the light?

Little vixen nosing among the stardust,
Chasing comets across the fields of space,
Out-foxing Orion, coaxing Cassiopeia
Into a dance – a volta, a galliard –
In strict time to the music of the spheres,
Digging through black holes, red dwarves, white
    giants.

FIONA RICHARDSON

What fiery worms and diamonds
Will she find in the heart of a nebula?

As above, so below, little vixen -
Show us your treasures.

the parrot

VICTORIA MINEVA

I found a new lover
It is the parrot
He fell in love at first sight
But I could reciprocate him not
He gave me his foot
And shared his food
I gave him a cookie
We understood
Perfectly each other
But we are not the same kind
But still, there was love
I gave him my hands up
And he sang me a song
That made me realize
He took my heart's spot
By giving me happiness
I almost forgot

it's funny what
people will say &
do to relate to one
another

WHITNEE COY

Her purple-hued legs, as long as my fingers
& the tubes that ran throughout her body
were as thick as her pine-needle arms.

When you explain to people
your baby is in the NICU, they never know what
    to say.
Prattle about a baby they once knew
who survived or read about
in a Facebook post. They preach phrases like
    "normal,"
"you'd never know," "even graduated early," or
"only had a hole in their heart" to make you feel
    relieved.
Jostle, how lucky you are & how thankful
you should feel. Your baby will be fine, & these
    moments
will pass when you can't hold her, feed her,
    bathe her,
touch her petal-thick skin that you once grew.

Curious people ask if her eyesight
will be okay & I wonder if oxygen

lines will snake through her nose forever.
Or pry if she will always be so tiny - can she
    catch up?
All I can think of is that because she was born
so young, she hadn't learned the reflex of suckling
& swallowing. No matter how many breastfeeding
    articles I read,
it would never matter as a toothpick-sized orange
feeding tube winds through her nose for nearly 45
    days.

It's funny what people will say &
do to relate to one another.

When in the dark of night, while everyone rests
& IVs streak both of your arms, you cry
with no sound, so nurses or your husband
    don't hear
because you should be thankful you survived.
She survived.
But your body feels empty
& your arms pine to hold her
foot-long body next to yours in rough
patterned hospital sheets.

Instead, in the quiet beeps of hospital rooms
you grieve the dreams you had
for your pregnancy, birth, & the beginning
days of her life.

Grief's like heavy weights
tied to your feet as you learn to walk again,
shuffle one foot after another
to the NICU in the morning light.

BARBARA ANN MEIER HOLTZ

I watch the birds flit in and out of spalling cracks of
    limestone,
wondering if they nest already in February?
The waitress serves my Belgian waffle with 2 per-
    fectly fried eggs.
Between bites I observe the building
sinking in on its foundation across the street.
I am sure if I went inside
there would be cracks starting to split walls.
The front facade with the degenerating
    "Team" sign
holds up the metal roof.

The waitress asks me if I need anything else and I
    smile and say
"No."
then
" I'd like a cup of coffee to go."

Coffee to keep me company as I wander the streets
    and dirt roads.
The foundations of so many barns, sheds, and
    houses "splitting asunder".
Lives lost in the rubble of limestone history.

"Heresies distressed".[1]

The Word circles around and around.
The hymn that morning humming in my mind,
like my tires hum on the road heading north.

My focus shall be the tears I shed at night
to build houses in my future.
Houses where sparrows come to rest
and coffee is served every morning.

---

1. The Church's One Foundation, SJ Stone

communion

ELLEN S. ROMANO

Prove the yeast with water and a little sugar,
the bubbles and tang let you know it's alive.
Add the flour cup by cup
then knead for the time it takes to sing three fa-
    vorite songs
so that joy and sorrow and transcendence are
    folded into the dough.
Cover it, keep it warm, nurture its rising
then press it down when the time comes.
Have faith it will rise again.

When you take it from the oven cut a piece
for your child so you may feed his hunger
with the labor of your hands.
Share a loaf with your neighbor.
Eat at your table while the dog watches
and let her lick the butter from your fingers.

Yet, love, mere love, is beautiful indeed
And worthy of acceptation. Fire is bright,
Let temple burn, or flax; an equal light
Leaps in the flame from cedar-plank or weed:
And love is fire. And when I say at need
I love thee ... mark! ... I love thee—in thy sight
I stand transfigured, glorified aright,
With conscience of the new rays that proceed
Out of my face toward thine. There's nothing low
In love, when love the lowest: meanest creatures
Who love God, God accepts while loving so.
And what I feel, across the inferior features
Of what I am, doth flash itself, and show
How that great work of Love enhances Nature's.

as the days pass faster

CASEY LAWRENCE

One day,
a long time ago,
I read that because time seems to pass more
      quickly
as you get older,
you've lived more than fifty percent of your life
by the time you turn twenty-one.

Days turn into hours
turn into minutes
turn into a camera flash,
a single moment frozen in a frame
on the mantel.

Just yesterday
you were celebrating your first wedding an-
      niversary
and now six — ten — twenty-five years
have gone by
in a blink.

The kitchen décor you chose together
has gone out of style.
That trendy velvet couch

is worn threadbare
in the spot where you sit
every day.

I do not have a monopoly on sorrow.
I press the heels of my palms to my eyes
and feel thankful that I am no soldier on the Front;
the gunshots are all in my head.

No medals of bravery are handed out
for going to the bakery, darning socks,
writing a novel, putting wine in a bucket of ice to
    chill,
losing the kitchen scissors, pumping a gallon
    of gas,
or wrapping Christmas presents.

Taking inventory of my life,
I feast on the crumbs
that have fermented in my brain,
growing stronger as time passes,
more poignant, not stale:

A birthday cake
with ten candles.

New Year's fireworks
at Lakeside Park.

Knees skinned
on the gravel driveway.

A first kiss
after midnight.

Elastic bands
tied in a chain.

I am not saintly.

From my roost above it all,
the soulful harmony of mistakes
and stolen moments strike discord,
add a bitter taste to the yesterdays:

I jabber during the movie
and miss the big reveal.

The half-finished puzzle
is left on the dining table for weeks.

Ornery bickering
about the laundry.

The bang of the screen door
slamming.

A cold shoulder,
an unshed tear.

Unanswered
text messages.

Time undulates in slow waves,
but the moments themselves
are drops of water.
You try to catch them,
but they slip from your fingers.

Suddenly, every politician has the same face.
You've seen that actress in something before
— but what?
You IMDB the good parts,
search Facebook albums
for the dates and places you swore never to forget.

We kissed on the ramparts, once.
Where?

How could we have lived in that apartment
for two years?
I don't remember
the carpet, the layout,
the cupboard handles.

I feel the sun on my face and worry
about wrinkles and melanoma,
but also think of it being my last chance
to feel the sun on my face,
and let it burn a while longer.

There are days I hate this world, this life.
Others, I am terrified of it being over too soon.
A single moment stolen from me:
there are really so few,
when you think about it.

How many more hugs from my mother?
How many more sunrises,
or sunsets,
will I see?

I am still young, I think.
The days still seem long,
sometimes.

The days are long
but the years speed by.
I worry about having enough time
for it all.

slough

JUDY CLARENCE

The golden goo
that forms when wounds
don't heal. Also mud
or mire. A swamp. A plodding
through that marsh or tide.
An easing off of work.
A creeping laziness. The job
does not get done.
The stuff that sluffs off
a snake that's shed. A mass
of dead moult, skin or goop
or muck that sucks itself down
into depths of ground or lake
or a deep incision. Down, down
into my leg until, surprised,
it finds the bone.

the whore

AN 18TH CENTURY POEM — PRICE
ONE SHILLING

AN HONEST WHORE

THANKS to the age, the satyrizing Muse
Has themes sufficient—where she will to chuse;
Whither among the vulgar scenes of strife,
Or those renown'd for Vice in higher life.
Lord, Duke, or Duchess, might the theme enhance,
And shew the worst of crimes—without romance.
St. James's, or *St. Giles*'s, will supply
Enough of subjects—in Iniquity.
WHORE is my theme, ye sisters all attend,
Give your applause, and be a sister's friend;
If this ye do, and cast a fav'ring eye,
Those Sons of Whores, the Critics, I defy.

Of all the crimes condemn'd in women-kind,
Whore, in the catalogue, the first you'll find;
This vulgar term is in the mouth of all
An epithet, on every female's fall.
And what's a Whore? Go ask the nations round;
Is it an empty name, and nought but sound?
Is it, above all other sins, the worst?
By man despised, and by God accurs'd?
If that's the case, and scripture we believe,
What was the crime alledg'd to grandam Eve?
What was the fruit the Tree of Knowledge shew'd,

And made her break her promise to her God?
What in the serpent could o'er her prevail;
Was the great evil in his head or tail?
The Devil himself must clear up the dispute,
Who knew the virtue of the fatal fruit.

But what's a WHORE in life?—pray let us find,
If possible we can, among mankind.
A woman, who the worst of thoughts debase,
All void of shame, of decency, and grace;
One who for hire her person will dispose,
And take, for need, each passer-by that goes.

Is, then, necessity the only plea?
Ye sisters in high life, come tell to me;
High fed, high bred, high marry'd too, indeed,
Do you not sometimes *whore* to mend the breed?
Necessity, with you, can have no claim;
Wants you have none—unless you know *that same*;
Your spouse, perhaps, lies snoring all the night,
While you are wishing for the soft delight.
Is impotence the case?—he old, you young,
Weak in his back, while you are stout and strong;
If he can't eat, pray why should you be starv'd?
The *craving Womb of Nature* must be serv'd.

This Newton knew, and like a cunning elf,
As spousy could not carve—she help'd herself.

But Grosv'nor, what could be the case with you?
'Good lack! my lord was to my bed untrue;
'Where'er he went he sought some lew'd embrace,
'Neglected me for ev'ry newer face;
'In silence long I mourn'd my hapless fate,
'At length determin'd to retaliate.
'Yet to no mean amour did I descend;
'A Prince my lover, and a Prince my friend.
'Who would not wish for such a lot as mine?
'Who would not be a *royal concubine?*

'Envy'd by ev'ry lady I could see,
'Who, if not WHORES, would fain be so—like me.'
And yet, mistaken Grosvenor, you find
His royal vows and oaths were all but wind;
He's satisfied himself, and comes no more,
While for your comfort—you've the name of
    WHORE.

Poor Ligonier was, too, condemn'd by fate
To find at last an insufficient mate;
One who could not her eager joys pursue,
And *pleasures standard* raise unto the view;
Therefore the staff she took into her hand,
And had a reg'ment at her own command.

Worsley, of late, has prov'd strong Nature's bent,
And try'd with many—for her own content;
Her willing cuckold she has nicely bam'd,
Who, for his vile compliance, should be d——d.
The meanest scoundrel, sure, in human life,
Is he who to another lets his wife;
Or basely does at lustful acts connive,
That he may *tippers* to his *horns* contrive;
Plead ign'rance, tho' he knows it all the while,
That his *wife*'s *friend*, of gold, he may beguile.

But say you, 'Spouses thus might be in fault;'
Consider what good lessons you'd been taught;
From earliest youth what tutors you have had,
That you might rise the joy of Mam and Dad;
Virtue and Prudence, names of mighty force,
You work'd upon your samplers of course;
No sights unseemly ever struck your eyes,
But all was done to make you good and wise.
'Twas, sure, the *force of Nature!* that was all,
Which thus could make your dignities to fall.
Had you been brought up in some foreign land,
Where sacred monast'ries around expand,
Such *slipp'ry tricks* you surely ne'er had done,

Each in her mind, no doubt, had been a Nun.

Of that I doubt, from stories I have heard,
And one I've ready for you now prepar'd.

A tender Virgin, by her *Parents* will,
(And virgins must their parents hopes fulfil)
Was to a cloyster in her bloom consign'd,
(Tho' she had no such wishes in her mind)
To fast and pray, instead of patch and paint,
And to be—God knows how, a very saint;
Join her soft voice unto the organ's note,
And all her thoughts to Heav'n alone must float;
The shadowy veil must hide her lovely face,
Where joy sat smiling with each charming grace;
Knees bent, eyes lifted, hands in order join'd,
Must shew her purest sanctity of mind.

Yet all this discipline was ill bestow'd,
Her youthful mind still thought of flesh and blood;
And, to conceal it, still she strove in vain;
She often in her cell would loud complain
How hard the lot insisted to obey,
And wish'd some man would steal her soon away;
More than her beads she then would him adore,
And be contented with the name of WHORE.

The Abbess heard her as she pass'd by chance,
And fancy'd she had got some vile romance;
Knock'd at the cell, and found her daughter there,
With not a book—unless a book of pray'r;
She wonder'd much, and told the virgin so,
Who did not hide the truth, but let her know.
Amaz'd the matron lifted up her eyes,
And shew'd her horror by her vast surprize.

'O! shame to all that's pious and that's good,
'What wild-fire's this which rages in your blood;
''Tis, sure, dictated by some imp of Hell!

'You must be mad!—Pray tell me, Are you well?
'Your understanding must be gone astray;
'I'll call the Doctor to you.—Well-a-day!'

The Nun persisted that her mind was right,
That she was in her perfect senses quite;
And Nature, in her wishes, still prevail'd.
Love fill'd her thoughts—and that was all that
    ail'd.

Again the pious Abbess strove, in vain,
Her wicked wants and wishes to explain;
Bid her take pattern by her sister Prue,
Who was to holy exercises true;
Who ne'er at morn. or evening pray'r, was found
To cast one carnal eye or thought around?
But ev'ry sense was calm, each wish was even,
And all her joy, and all her hope in Heav'n.

The tender maiden look'd again and sigh'd,
And to her mental mother thus reply'd:—

'Prue, that you mention, as I've heard her say,
'Was, in her younger days, entic'd away;
'The strong temptation she could not withstand,
'But yielded up at *Nature*'s high command.
'Long with a youth in *dalliance* pass'd her life,
'Had all the joys of love—tho' not a wife;
'And when he left her for a real bride,
'She did another for herself provide;
'Another after that, when that was gone,
'And so, for many years, in joy went on;
''Till tir'd of *sporting* in the am'rous way,
'She turn'd a *Nun*, at last, to fast and pray.
'By her example let me then proceed;
'On joy and pleasure let my wishes feed;
'And when that I've been cloy'd with love like her,
'Pray'rs, and a Nunnery, I may prefer.'

Was not the Virgin, tell me sisters pure,
Within her mind a HARLOT?—Certain sure.

Such, in our boarding-schools, we often find,
Where, to improve their morals, they're design'd:
Yet Lewdness, there, is found among the train,
And Virtue faintly does her rights maintain;
The Dancing-Master, and the Frizeur too,
The *pleasing sports* of Venus bring to view;
Big bellies and *elopements* will take place,
And WHORES alike be found in ev'ry place.

But why, by me can never be devis'd,
A WHORE should be so horridly despis'd;
Why, when by all, throughout the world, they're
    us'd!
Why they should be so cruelly abus'd.

The pulpit-thumper rails against a WHORE,
And damns the Prostitute!—What can he more?
Justice pursues her to the very cart,
Where, for her folly, she is doom'd to smart.
Whips, Gaols, Diseases! all the WHORE assail,
And yet, I fancy, WHORES will never fail.

What is the reason WHORES are so in vogue?
Why, faith, to gain a true one, ask each Rogue.

The very Priest, who dares so much decry,
And holds his doctrine up so very high,
Will, from the pulpit, cast a side-long glance,
To damn the tenets which he dares advance;
And e'er, perhaps, he goes to evening pray'r,
Will take a bottle with some willing fair;
Will to her breasts his saint-like hands apply,
And gaze upon her with lascivious eye,
In pleasure's pulpit then will mount, and preach
A forceful doctrine, which he dares not teach;
Then, sanctify'd, will to his flock amain,

Hem, stroke his band—and rail at WHORES
    again.

The Justice too, who puts the laws in force,
Must seem a tyrant over us, of course;
Produce each hum-drum act, from bad to worse,
Made by old fumblers, for the HARLOT's curse.
Bridewell's the sentence, then, to all who're poor,
But, *gold well tipp'd*, will save the *flashy* WHORE;
And the good magistrate some clause will find
To soften evidence unto his mind;
Perhaps at night, considering the case,
Indulge his feelings in a close embrace;
Will, at the tavern, circulate his glass,
And take, with glee, his bottle and his lass.

Go to the *Commons*[1], to the *Arches* go,
Where, for divorces, people sue, we know.
The Judges and the Proctors, so devout,
Would, with the culprit, wish to have a bout.
Adultery, tho' call'd a crying sin,
Without they're paid, would not be worth a pin:
They'll sell you licences to get a bride,
And, on complaint, divorces have beside.
O happy land! where such good laws remain,
That you may wed, and be unwed again;
That sacred knot, recorded so on high!
Those who have money may with ease untie;
Yet there's no sister ever this deplores,
Because it adds so to the list of WHORES.

Ask at that place where Lords and Commons sit,
To shew at once their eloquence and wit;
Who rule the nation, and its laws provide,
Lift high our fame, the legislation guide;
From the Right Rev'rend, in the prelate's place,
The noble Count, or more exalted Grace:
Or of the members on the lower side,
Whose consequence by none can be deny'd;

Ask F——x and S———dw——h; aye, and many
   more,
If they, at times, have each not had a WHORE?

The question's foolish, ev'ry one must guess
They all are guilty—either more or less!
Were they but stigmatiz'd, as women are,
Condemn'd a load of infamy to bear,
Their Honours, and Right Honourables too,
Would fear to bring their faces forth to view.
Why then should we be thus condemn'd alone,
When they are guilty, equal, ev'ry one;
Were there no men, no WHORES there sure
   could be,
They strive to make us so, in each degree.

Have we a face that's exquisitely fair,
They spread their nets, that beauty to ensnare;
Is modesty and innocence our guide,
To try to ruin it is all their pride;
If we are humble, they our hopes will raise,
Strive to undo us still, a thousand ways;
Gold, flattery, and treach'ry, they employ,
The object which delights them to destroy;
Then cast aside, neglected or forgot,
We're doom'd to pine, to languish, and to rot:
Or if, when such delusive arts are o'er,
We go to others—each is then a WHORE!

Ye Rogues of Fortune, and ye Rogues of Pow'r,
Who ruin females in the guardless hour;
Who may be Sons of WHORES, for what you know,
Attend to what my artless pen can shew.

Not far from Town, and in a rural place,
Where Nature shone with ev'ry pleasing grace;
Where rising hills gave rapture to the sight,
With flocks, whose fleeces were all snowy white;
Beneath, where lawns extended wide around,

And silver murm'ring rivulets were found;
There in a humble, tho' not mean, estate,
I drew my being, as ordain'd by fate.
My parents, tho' not born to wealth and pride,
The markets still with various things supply'd;
Industrious both, they happ'ly found the gains
Were equal to their wishes and their pains.
I was their only child, and form'd to bless,
I always added to their happiness;
They saw my person ev'ry one engage,
Beheld my sense increasing with my age;
Each Sunday to my dress they'd something add,
For pleasing me was making of them glad;
A diff'rent ribband bound my flowing hair,
Wav'd in my hat, and flutter'd in the air;
Thus simply pleas'd, and innocent likewise,
I caught, at last, Lothario's wanton eyes.

About fifteen, my face had Nature's bloom,
My lips enticing, and my breath perfume!
My eyes, like sloes, were glossy, black, and bright!
My shape was slender, and my steps were light!

He saw me tripping o'er the dewy lawn,
Brisk as the lambkins, or the bounding fawn;
He hail'd my beauties in so soft a speech,
Which sure a heart less kind than mine might
    reach;
I blush'd, he follow'd, met me ev'ry day,
'Till I became, at last, his destin'd prey.
Yet, oh! what vows, what oaths, did he prepare,
Before I fell into his baneful snare;
He call'd me wife, swore I should be his bride,
With protestations, very high beside;
Beg'd to my parents I would nothing tell,
If that I wish'd his love and person well.

His friends were pow'rful, and I soon comply'd,
For what he ask'd, then could not be deny'd;

I thought that time would reconcile my fate,
And lift me far above my present state;
Such fatal folly I must still deplore,
No wife am I, but a neglected WHORE!

Fruition soon my lover's passion cool'd,
His absence let me know how I was fool'd;
My heaving womb a diff'rent weight confest,
My parents saw it, and were much distrest:
I told the cause;—they turn'd me out of door,
And made we wander forth a wretched WHORE!

To faithless him my ruin I must lay,
He first seduc'd and did my heart betray:—
High in a diff'rent sphere he took a wife;
O! may she be to him eternal strife;
May she to lustful passion give her heart!
That ev'ry fool, with him, may have a part;
Tho' higher born, no diff'rence I can see
She should not be a WHORE—as well as me.
That WHORES are many, certainly you'll find,
Is owing to the baseness of mankind;
Tho' inclination oft' our passions sway,
'Tis man, vile man! first teaches us the way.

By him we first are taught each vicious art,
Each crime which can corrupt and spoil the heart.
Is any female fond of dress, or play,
(And where is one that is not?—you will say)
Her fav'rite passion he will strive to please,
And work into her folly by degrees;
Like vermin in a building, undermine,
'Till the whole pile falls down—his whole design;
Then leaves the ruin he himself has made,
Without one spark of gratitude display'd.

No pitying eye beholds the hapless fair,
She's left to Death, Diseases, and Despair!
Nature cries out, and hunger must be fed,

She now must turn a prostitute for bread;
Her name is blasted, friendless left, and poor,
Tell me what can she do?—why be a WHORE.
Lew'd scenes, and lew'd discourse, comes next in
        play;
Deeds dark as night, asham'd to meet the day!
Thus they proceed along, from bad to worse,
Launch the broad oath! repeat the dreadful curse!
'Till, on a laystall, she resigns her breath,
By all unpityed, to the arms of death!

Yet ev'ry one of feeling must deplore,
That man, vile man, first made the wretch a
        WHORE!

------

1. Doctor's Commons.

i walked with my eyes closed

ELLEN S. ROMANO

I Walked With My Eyes Closed
in the halls of this school
our sons once attended,
where I spent years
teaching other people's children.

Alert to the subtle changes of light
that meant I was passing a window,
I counted out my steps, never passing twenty
before opening my eyes
for a quick look, a readjustment.

It was peaceful once to walk
in self-imposed blindness early in the morning
before the students arrived
or in the sudden quiet at the end of the day.

I imagined myself walking over
the footsteps our children once made
in this place where I first came as a young mother,
then walked into old age.

Now I move only toward your remembered image,

giving meaning to all my practice.
A specter of you waits at the end of the hallway.
Am I getting closer? You will only stay
until I open my eyes. I count each step,
twenty-one, twenty-two, twenty-three.

learning slowly

PULKITA ANAND

One day the unheard sounds great
One day the unnoticed shimmers
One day the unloved is a darling
One day the uncared is precious
One day the uncharted beckons
My God woke up with me and walked
And worked at the workstation
Sipped coffee and missed the sunrise
with me
Though others say the contrary
But I know this is where I have to go
This is where the soul exults to eat and dance
Learn to live with the loneliness within us
Let the sun ride its horses
Let the rain stitch the soul

collector of things

BAILEY GREY

I'm a collector of things
Pursuer of mementos
Pre and current and post nostalgia
My memories are now.

In the sleeves of my silk purple robe,
In the stillness of my painting of a seal in a
    party hat,
In the broken button on my orange floral
    dungarees.

Everything is consciousness
And we all tell a story.
I melt these memories with utmost rigour--
Into my soul of chaos.

I'm a Collector of Things,
Of Summertime flings,
An overdue copy of I Know why the Caged Bird
    Sings.

If I had the choice,
See, I'd rather have wings.
But here I stand, a collector of things.

What does it mean,
To have a cluttered apartment?
I am no hoarder,
And-
Yet,
I enjoy the clutter,
The abundance of stuff--
Of memories,
Of all time happening now.

Collector of things,
Lover of this life,
The next one,
And the previous one, too.

I'm a collector of things,
A patron of *pings*,
Bury me with Richard Sherman's granddaughter's
     ring.
To my Caledonian Sleeper Train towel, I shall cling.

Stuff in my soul boxes,
Faith's old pink T -shirt,
The one she gave me when we were [the closest of]
     friends.
In my frame of knowledge,
Nothing ever truly ends.

I am a collector,
A protector,
A friend.
A lover.
A daughter.
A soul.

I am a collector of things.

ALEXANDRIA TANNENBAUM

At thirteen, you always slouched.
You read once in a teen magazine
slouching made your arms appear thinner,
(moved away from your body,)
suspended in air like a bridge.

You smiled with lips sealed
to hide the way teeth made room

for shadows when you spoke

never showed your ears
because once a boy said they stuck out
when you dared to lift the curtain
of your hair...

you're

my

little elf,

he said,

took a rock to carve it into the
science table where you traced the
tracks with the tip of your finger,
embarrassed at the permanence
of this confusing act.

You always slouched

to appear smaller,

so when the boys at school
wanted to throw orange peels
up your skirt at lunch,
pebbled and torn by teeth,
or snap the bra your mom
helped to pick out,
they wouldn't notice the way you
burrowed into the earth of the day,
staying far from sun
as dirt crumbled
around makeshift walls.

They made a list

of the hottest girls at school,
told your twelve-year-old-self
it was a compliment–

you

should

be flattered–

listed which body part they liked the most.
You, fingernail paint chipping
tucked away the folded proof
against your thigh
carried it to every class.

Yes, your name will fade away
the curvature of letters
folding into themselves

just as soon as you stop looking.

edward and josephine hopper: a love story in paint

SUZANNE MORRIS

The diminutive painter
known affectionately as Jo

wed the six-foot-four giant
when she was forty-one

surrendering her lyrical signature–
widely known by then–

though not her painting,
as many presumed,

her muse unruly as her
bushy auburn hair escaping its pins.

Early on, man and wife,
working side by side

painted a pair of church towers
on the Massachusetts coast.

Her flamboyant coloring
made the towers soar

blessed by Our Lady
of Good Voyage

while his left them
mortared firmly in place

peering through arched windows

from behind
a wooden fence.

Edward spent prolonged periods
hardly speaking to Jo

his head bent low over
minute details

of high mansard windows,
their awnings whipped by the wind

or darkness enveloping a
lonely corner drug store.

Jo, devoted to Edward's career,

stole time and space
in fleeting bouts:

pochades emerging in rapid strokes
from behind the car window.

Her figures were
chatty and gay,

champagne uncorked from the
picture plane;

his were standoffish
and morose

his meaning an enigma
as he famously portrayed

not what was there, but
what he wished to see.

Jo's canny advocacy brought
Edward the notice he craved

while her work went
largely forgotten.

Eddy, she called him, endearingly
whenever she was pleased;

E, whenever she was not,
which was the case more often.

His last oil painting is
said to convey

his perception of
the two as equal partners:

a pair of clown figures
in identical garb

taking a bow upon a
gaping proscenium stage.

How Jo had seen the pair, over
the long course of their marriage

was– perhaps for lack of time
and space–

a canvas primed, but
left unpainted.

. . .

Note: July 9th, 2024 marked the 100th anniversary of the marriage of Josephine Verstille Nivison and Edward Hopper.

on the benefits of cold water swimming

LINDA ROSEWOOD

I swim with some old ones at Portnablagh pier.
Each day at eleven, we gather.
The sky's often gray and the wind quite severe,
As into the water we swagger.

There's Orla and Aileen, Fiona and Ned,
Liam, and Aisling McBride,
Clare from Clonmore and Tim from Horn Head
We all miss Dermot, who died.

When I was young, I avoided the cold.
A behavior I sorely regret.
Now everything hurts, like it does when you're old
But I'll swim any water that's wet.

I shriek and go under the bone-chilling swell.
We all judge each other quite wacky.
I can't help but think of death and farewell
Like always I do when I'm happy.

The days they pass by inevitably,
But dark nights cause me no fear.
When the final tide turns, my last memory will be
Swimming into the sun at the pier.

drunken drama teacher

JUDITH SKILLMAN

Still under sloeblack Dylan Thomas' words pour
from his beer mouth Llaregubb, "bugger all"
he invites me into the prop room full of manikins
wooded area in the hills we fall deep in beer cans
clatter of Welsh I'm raped different Rosie Probert
some dandelion seeded on Coronation Street
or near the River Dewi don't Organ Morgan love
    his Bach
where'd my bloom go now I'm walking offstage
curtained hair mane in a tall territory
night-haunted sometimes asleep

everything

HOLLY PAYNE-STRANGE

What if everything
Goes well?

What if today is perfect,
And we laugh, and hug and play,
Holding each others hearts gently,
Carefully, like some revered treasure
From a civilization long ago?

What if every word we say is magic?
Discovering the correct phrasing
As if excavating some magnificent temple,
Gold and emeralds shimmering on our lips.

What if you re-discover happiness today?
Maybe just a little
The very first chords
Of some blissful melody,
A new and thrilling tune.
Or
A familiar refrain,
A deep and ancient hum
That fills your bones and never let's go?

It's possible. Maybe even probable.

Come with me
And I have a feeling we can make it
True.

his right hook / isaiah 46

BARBARA ANN MEIER HOLTZ

They build a city for an idol,
with tables of destiny
like Nebo's clay tablets,
where he dispenses his wisdom,
even though he cannot stroll the streets,
speak the answers we seek,
or spare us the Cyrus' in our lives.
Idols can be shoplifted,
ripped from walls,
smashed by battle axes,
becoming the crushing weight
on an onager's back,
Clay on stone,
iron on feet,
where the God you cannot steal,
has set the pins,
sparing no one
the bowling balls
thrown with His right hook.

apocalypse

EMILY DICKINSON

I'm wife; I've finished that,
That other state;
I'm Czar, I'm woman now:
It's safer so.

How odd the girl's life looks
Behind this soft eclipse!
I think that earth seems so
To those in heaven now.

This being comfort, then
That other kind was pain;
But why compare?
I'm wife! stop there!

the sleep wind

SAPPHO

TRANSLATED BY H. DE VERE
STACPOOLE

Softer than mists o'er the pale green of waters,
O'er the charmed sea, shod with sandals of shadow
Comes the warm sleep wind of Argolis, floating
Garlands of fragrance;

Comes the sweet wind by the still hours attended,
Touching tired lids on the shores dim with
    distance,
Ever its way toward the headland of Lesbos,
Toward Mitylene.

Faintly one fair star of evening enkindles
On the dusk afar its lone fire Œtean,
Shining serene till the darkness will deepen
Others to splendor;

Bringing ineffable peace, and the gladsome
Return with the night of all things that morning
Ruthlessly parted, the child to its mother,
Lover to lover.

From the marble court of rose-crowned com-
    panions,
All alone my feet again seek the little

Theatre pledged to the Muse, now deserted,
Facing the surges;

Where the carved Pan-heads that laugh down the
    gentle
Slope of broad steps to the refluent ripple,
Flute from their thin pipes the dithyrambs
    deathless,
Songs all unuttered.

Empty each seat where my girl friends acclaimed
    me,
Poets with names on the tiered stone engraven,
Over whose verge blooms the apple tree, drifting
Perfume and petals;

Gone Telesippa and tender Gyrinno,
Anactoria, woman divine; Atthis,
Subtlest of soul, fair Damophyla, Dica,
Maids of the Muses.

Here an hour past soul-enravished they listened
While my rapt heart breathed its pæan im-
    passioned,
Chanted its wild prayer to thee, Aphrodite,
Daughter of Cyprus;

Now to their homes are they gone in the city,
Pensive to dream limb-relaxed while the languid
Slaves come and lift from the tresses they loosen,
Flowers that have faded.

Thou alone, Sappho, art sole with the silence,
Sole with night and dreams that are darkness,
    weaving
Thoughts that are sighs from the heart and their
    meaning
Vague as the shadow;

When the great silence shall come to thee, sad one,
Men that forget shall remember thy music,
Murmur thy name that shall steal on their passion
Soft as the sleep wind.

a little called pauline

GERTRUDE STEIN

A LITTLE CALLED anything shows shudders.

Come and say what prints all day. A whole few water-melon. There is no pope.

No cut in pennies and little dressing and choose wide soles and little spats really little spices.

A little lace makes boils. This is not true.

Gracious of gracious and a stamp a blue green white bow a blue green lean, lean on the top.

If it is absurd then it is leadish and nearly set in where there is a tight head.

A peaceful life to arise her, noon and moon and moon. A letter a cold sleeve a blanket a shaving house and nearly the best and regular window.

Nearer in fairy sea, nearer and farther, show white has lime in sight, show a stitch of ten. Count, count more so that thicker and thicker is leaning.

I hope she has her cow. Bidding a wedding, widening received treading, little leading mention nothing.

Cough out cough out in the leather and really feather it is not for.

Please could, please could, jam it not plus more sit in when.

admetus

TO MY FRIEND, RALPH WALDO
EMERSON

EMMA LAZARUS

He who could beard the lion in his lair,
To bind him for a girl, and tame the boar,
And drive these beasts before his chariot,
Might wed Alcestis. For her low brows' sake,
Her hairs' soft undulations of warm gold,
Her eyes clear color and pure virgin mouth,
Though many would draw bow or shiver spear,
Yet none dared meet the intolerable eye,
Or lipless tusk, of lion or boar.
This heard Admetus, King of Thessaly,
Whose broad, fat pastures spread their ample
    fields
Down to the sheer edge of Amphrysus' stream,
Who laughed, disdainful, at the father's pride,
That set such value on one milk-faced child.
One morning, as he rode alone and passed
Through the green twilight of Thessalian woods,
Between two pendulous branches interlocked,
As through an open casement, he descried
A goddess, as he deemed,—in truth a maid.
On a low bank she fondled tenderly
A favorite hound, her floral face inclined
above the glossy, graceful animal,
That pressed his snout against her cheek and gazed

Wistfully, with his keen, sagacious eyes.
One arm with lax embrace the neck enwreathed,
With polished roundness near the sleek, gray skin.
Admetus, fixed with wonder, dare not pass,
Intrusive on her holy innocence
And sacred girlhood, but his fretful steed
Snuffed the air, and champed and pawed the
     ground;
And hearing this, the maiden raised her head.
No let or hindrance then might stop the king,
Once having looked upon those supreme eyes.
The drooping boughs disparting, forth he sped,
And then drew in his steed, to ask the path,
Like a lost traveller in an alien land.
Although each river-cloven vale, with streams
Arrowy glancing to the blue Aegean,
Each hallowed mountain, the abode of gods,
Pelion and Ossa fringed with haunted groves,
The height, spring-crowned, of dedicate Olympus,
And pleasant sun-fed vineyards, were to him
Familiar as his own face in the stream,
Nathless he paused and asked the maid what path
Might lead him from the forest. She replied,
But still he tarried, and with sportsman's praise
Admired the hound and stooped to stroke its head,
And asked her if she hunted. Nay, not she:
Her father Pelias hunted in these woods,
Where there was royal game. He knew her now,

———

Alcestis,—and he left her with due thanks:
No goddess, but a mortal, to be won
By such a simple feat as driving boars
And lions to his chariot. What was that
To him who saw the boar of Calydon,
The sacred boar of Artemis, at bay
In the broad stagnant marsh, and sent his darts
In its tough, quivering flank, and saw its death,
Stung by sure arrows of Arcadian nymph?
To river-pastures of his flocks and herds

Admetus rode, where sweet-breathed cattle
    grazed,
Heifers and goats and kids, and foolish sheep
Dotted cool, spacious meadows with bent heads,
And necks' soft wool broken in yellow flakes,
Nibbling sharp-toothed the rich, thick-growing
    blades.
One herdsman kept the innumerable droves—
A boy yet, young as immortality—
In listless posture on a vine-grown rock.
Around him huddled kids and sheep that left
The mother's udder for his nighest grass,
Which sprouted with fresh verdure where he sat.
And yet dull neighboring rustics never guessed
A god had been among them till he went,
Although with him they acted as he willed,
Renouncing shepherds' silly pranks and quips,
Because his very presence made them grave.
Amphryssius, after their translucent stream,
They called him, but Admetus knew his name,—
Hyperion, god of sun and song and silver speech,
Condemned to serve a mortal for his sin
To Zeus in sending violent darts of death,
A raising hand irreverent, against
The one-eyed forgers of the thunderbolt.
For shepherd's crook he held the living rod
Of twisted serpents, later Hermes' wand.
Him sought the king, discovering soon hard by,
Idle as one in nowise bound to time,
Watching the restless grasses blow and wave,
The sparkle of the sun upon the stream,
Regretting nothing, living with the hour:
For him, who had his light and song within,
Was naught that did not shine, and all things sang.
Admetus prayed for his celestial aid
To win Alcestis, which the god vouchsafed,
Granting with smiles, as grant all gods, who smite
With stern hand, sparing not for piteousness,
But give their gifts in gladness.

Thus the king
Led with loose rein the beasts as tame as kine,
And townsfolk thronged within the city streets,
As round a god; and mothers showed their babes,
And maidens loved the crowned intrepid youth,
And men aloud worship, though the very god
Who wrought the wonder dwelled unnoted nigh,
Divinely scornful of neglect or praise.
Then Pelias, seeing this would be his son,
As he had vowed, called for his wife and child.
With Anaxibia, Alcestis came,
A warm flush spreading o'er her eager face
In looking on the rider of the woods,
And knowing him her suitor and the king.
Admetus won Alcestis thus to wife,
And these with mated hearts and mutual love
Lived a life blameless, beautiful: the king
Ordaining justice in the gates; the queen,
With grateful offerings to the household gods,
Wise with the wisdom of the pure in heart.
One child she bore,—Eumelus,—and he throve.
Yet none the less because they sacrificed
The firstlings of their flocks and fruits and flowers,
Did trouble come; for sickness seized the king.
Alcestis watched with many-handed love,
But unavailing service, for he lay
With languid limbs, despite his ancient strength
Of sinew, and his skill with spear and sword.
His mother came, Clymene, and with her
His father, Pheres: his unconscious child
They brought him, while forlorn Alcestis sat
Discouraged, with the face of desolation.
The jealous gods would bind his mouth from
    speech,
And smite his vigorous frame with impotence;
And ruin with bitter ashes, worms, and dust,
The beauty of his crowned, exalted head.
He knew her presence,—soon he would not know,
Nor feel her hand in his lie warm and close,

Nor care if she were near him any more.
Exhausted with long vigils, thus the queen
Held hard and grievous thoughts, till heavy sleep
Possessed her weary sense, and she dreamed.
And even in her dream her trouble lived,
For she was praying in a barren field
To all the gods for help, when came across
The waste of air and land, from distant skies,
A spiritual voice divinely clear,
Whose unimaginable sweetness thrilled
Her aching heart with tremor of strange joy:
"Arise, Alcestis, cast away white fear.
A god dwells with you: seek, and you shall find."
Then quiet satisfaction filled her soul
Almost akin to gladness, and she woke.
Weak as the dead, Admetus lay there still;
But she, superb with confidence, arose,
And passed beyond the mourners' curious eyes,
Seeking Amphryssius in the meadow-lands.
She found him with the godlike mien of one
Who, roused, awakens unto deeds divine:
"I come, Hyperion, with incessant tears,
To crave the life of my dear lord the king.
Pity me, for I see the future years
Widowed and laden with disastrous days.
And ye, the gods, will miss him when the fires
Upon your shrines, unfed, neglected die.
Who will pour large libations in your names,
And sacrifice with generous piety?
Silence and apathy will greet you there
Where once a splendid spirit offered praise.
Grant me this boon divine, and I will beat
With prayer at morning's gates, before they ope
Unto thy silver-hoofed and flame-eyed steeds.
Answer ere yet the irremeable stream
Be crossed: answer, O god, and save!"
She ceased,
With full throat salt with tears, and looked on him,
And with a sudden cry of awe fell prone,

For, lo! he was transmuted to a god;
The supreme aureole radiant round his brow,
Divine refulgences on his face,—his eyes
Awful with splendor, and his august head
With blinding brilliance crowned by vivid flame.
Then in a voice that charmed the listening air:
"Woman, arise! I have no influence
On Death, who is the servant of the Fates.
Howbeit for thy passion and thy prayer,
The grace of thy fair womanhood and youth,
Thus godlike will I intercede for thee,
And sue the insatiate sisters for this life.
Yet hope not blindly: loth are these to change
Their purpose; neither will they freely give,
But haggling lend or sell: perchance the price
Will counterveil the boon. Consider this.
Now rise and look upon me." And she rose,
But by her stood no godhead bathed in light,
But young Amphryssius, herdsman to the king,
Benignly smiling.
Fleet as thought, the god
Fled from the glittering earth to blackest depths
Of Tartarus; and none might say he sped
On wings ambrosial, or with feet as swift
As scouring hail, or airy chariot
Borne by the flame-breathing steeds ethereal;
But with a motion inconceivable
Departed and was there. Before the throne
Of Ades, first he hailed the long-sought queen,
Stolen with violent hands from grassy fields
And delicate airs of sunlit Sicily,
Pensive, gold-haired, but innocent-eyed no more
As when she laughing plucked the daffodils,
But grave as on fulfilling a strange doom.
And low at Ades' feet, wrapped in grim murk
And darkness thick, the three gray women sat,
Loose-robed and chapleted with wool and flowers,
Purple narcissi round their horrid hair.
Intent upon her task, the first one held

The tender thread that at a touch would snap;
The second weaving it with warp and woof
Into strange textures, some stained dark and foul,
Some sanguine-colored, and some black as night,
And rare ones white, or with a golden thread
Running throughout the web: the farthest hag
With glistening scissors cut her sisters' work.
To these Hyperion, but they never ceased,
Nor raised their eyes, till with soft, moderate tones,
But by their powerful persuasiveness
Commanding all to listen and obey,
He spoke, and all hell heard, and these three looked
And waited his request:
I come, a god,
At pure mortal queen's request, who sues
For life renewed unto her dying lord,
Admetus; and I also pray this prayer."
"Then cease, for when hath Fate been moved by
        prayer?"
"But strength and upright heart should serve with
        you."
"I ask ye not forever to forbear,
But spare a while,—a moment unto us,
A lifetime unto men." "The Fates swerve not
For supplications, like the pliant gods.
Have they not willed a life's thread should be cut?
With them the will is changeless as the deed.
O men! ye have not learned in all the past,
Desires are barren and tears yield no fruit.
How long will ye besiege the thrones of gods
With lamentations? When lagged Death for all
Your timorous shirking? We work not like you,
Delaying and relenting, purposeless,
With unenduring issues; but our deeds,
Forever interchained and interlocked,
Complete each other and explain themselves."
"Ye will a life: then why not any life?"
"What care we for the king? He is not worth
These many words; indeed, we love not speech.

We care not if he live, or lose such life
As men are greedy for,—filled full with hate,
Sins beneath scorn, and only lit by dreams,
Or one sane moment, or a useless hope,—
Lasting how long?—the space between the green
And fading yellow of the grass they tread."
But he withdrawing not: "Will any life
Suffice ye for Admetus?" "Yea," the crones
Three times repeated. "We know no such names
As king or queen or slave: we want but life.
Begone, and vex us in our work no more."
With broken blessings, inarticulate joy
And tears, Alcestis thanked Hyperion,
And worshipped. Then he gently: "Who will die,
So that the king may live?" And she: "You ask?
Nay, who will live when life clasps hands with
        shame,
And death with honor? Lo, you are a god;
You cannot know the highest joy of life,—
To leave it when 't is worthier to die.
His parents, kinsmen, courtiers, subjects, slaves,—
For love of him myself would die, were none
Found ready; but what Greek would stand to see
A woman glorified, and falter? Once,
And only once, the gods will do this thing
In all the ages: such a man themselves
Delight to honor,—holy, temperate, chaste,
With reverence for his daemon and his god."
Thus she triumphant to they very door
Of King Admetus' chamber. All there saw
Her ill-timed gladness with much wonderment.
But she: "No longer mourn! The king is saved:
The Fates will spare him. Lift your voice in praise;
Sing paeans to Apollo; crown your brows
With laurel; offer thankful sacrifice!"
"O Queen, what mean these foolish words
        misplaced?
And what an hour is this to thank the Fates?"
"Thrice blessed be the gods!—for God himself

Has sued for me,—they are not stern and deaf.
Cry, and they answer: commune with your soul,
And they send counsel: weep with rainy grief,
And these will sweeten you your bitterest tears.
On one condition King Admetus lives,
And ye, on hearing, will lament no more,
Each emulous to save." Then—for she spake
Assured, as having heard an oracle—
They asked: "What deed of ours may serve the
    king?"
"The Fates accept another life for his,
And one of you may die." Smiling, she ceased.
But silence answered her. "What! do ye thrust
Your arrows in your hearts beneath your cloaks,
Dying like Greeks, too proud to own the pang?
This ask I not. In all the populous land
But one need suffer for immortal praise.
The generous Fates have sent no pestilence,
Famine, nor war: it is as though they gave
Freely, and only make the boon more rich
By such slight payment. Now a people mourns,
And ye may change the grief to jubilee,
Filling the cities with a pleasant sound.
But as for me, what faltering words can tell
My joy, in extreme sharpness kin to pain?
A monument you have within my heart,
Wreathed with kind love and dear remem-
    brances;
And I will pray for you before I crave
Pardon and pity for myself from God.
Your name will be the highest in the land,
Oftenest, fondest on my grateful lips,
After the name of him you die to save.
What! silent still? Since when has virtue grown
Less beautiful than indolence and ease?
Is death more terrible, more hateworthy,
More bitter than dishonor? Will ye live
On shame? Chew and find sweet its poisoned
    fruits?

What sons will ye bring forth—mean-souled
    like you,
Or, like your parents, brave—to blush like girls,
And say,'Our fathers were afraid to die!'
Ye will not dare to raise heroic eyes
Unto the eyes of aliens. In the streets
Will women and young children point at you
Scornfully, and the sun will find you shamed,
And night refuse to shield you. What a life
Is this ye spin and fashion for yourselves!
And what new tortures of suspense and doubt
Will death invent for such as are afraid!
Acastus, thou my brother, in the field
Foremost, who greeted me with sanguine hands
From ruddy battle with a conqueror's face,—
These honors wilt thou blot with infamy?
Nay, thou hast won no honors: a mere girl
Would do as much as thou at such a time,
In clamorous battle,'midst tumultuous sounds,
Neighing of war-steeds, shouts of sharp command,
Snapping of shivered spears; for all are brave
When all men look to them expectantly;
But he is truly brave who faces death
Within his chamber, at a sudden call,
At night, when no man sees,—content to die
When life can serve no longer those he loves."
Then thus Acastus: "Sister, I fear not
Death, nor the empty darkness of the grave,
And hold my life but as a little thing,
Subject unto my people's call, and Fate.
But if 't is little, no greater is the king's;
And though my heart bleeds sorely, I recall
Astydamia, who thus would mourn for me.
We are not cowards, we youth of Thessaly,
And Thessaly—yea, all Greece—knoweth it;
Nor will we brook the name from even you,
Albeit a queen, and uttering these wild words
Through your umwonted sorrow." Then she knew
That he stood firm, and turning from him, cried

To the king's parents: "Are ye deaf with grief,
Pheres, Clymene? Ye can save your son,
Yet rather stand and weep with barren tears.
O, shame! to think that such gray, reverend hairs
Should cover such unvenerable heads!
What would ye lose?—a remnant of mere life,
A few slight raveled threads, and give him years
To fill with glory. Who, when he is gone,
Will call you gentlest names this side of heaven,—
Father and mother? Knew ye not this man
Ere he was royal,—a poor, helpless child,
Crownless and kingdomless? One birth alone
Sufficeth not, Clymene: once again
You must give life with travail and strong pain.
Has he not lived to outstrip your swift hopes?
What mother can refuse a second birth
To such a son? But ye denying him,
What after-offering may appease the gods?
What joy outweigh the grief of this one day?
What clamor drown the hours' myriad tongues,
Crying, 'Your son, your son? where is your son,
Unnatural mother, timid foolish man?"
Then Pheres gravely: "These are graceless words
From you our daughter. Life is always life,
And death comes soon enough to such as we.
We twain are old and weak, have served our time,
And made our sacrifices. Let the young
Arise now in their turn and save the king."
"O gods! look on your creatures! do ye see?
And seeing, have ye patience? Smite them all,
Unsparing, with dishonorable death.
Vile slaves! a woman teaches you to die.
Intrepid, with exalted steadfast soul,
Scorn in my heart, and love unutterable,
I yield the Fates my life, and like a god
Command them to revere that sacred head.
Thus kiss I thrice the dear, blind, holy eyes,
And bid them see; and thrice I kiss this brow,
And thus unfasten I the pale, proud lips

With fruitful kissings, bringing love and life,
And without fear or any pang, I breathe
My soul in him."
"Alcestis, I awake.
I hear, I hear—unspeak thy reckless words!
For, lo! thy life-blood tingles in my veins,
And streameth through my body like new wine.
Behold! thy spirit dedicate revives
My pulse, and through thy sacrifice I breathe.
Thy lips are bloodless: kiss me not again.
Ashen thy cheeks, faded thy flower-like hands.
O woman! perfect in thy womanhood
And in thy wifehood, I adjure thee now
As mother, by the love thou bearest our child,
In this thy hour of passion and of love,
Of sacrifice and sorrow, to unsay
Thy words sublime!" "I die that thou mayest live."
"And deemest thou that I accept the boon,
Craven, like these my subjects? Lo, my queen,
Is life itself a lovely thing,—bare life?
And empty breath a thing desirable?
Or is it rather happiness and love
That make it precious to its inmost core?
When these are lost, are there not swords in
    Greece,
And flame and poison, deadly waves and plagues?
No man has ever lacked these things and gone
Unsatisfied. It is not these the gods refuse
(Nay, never clutch my sleeve and raise thy lip),—
Not these I seek; but I will stab myself,
Poison my life and burn my flesh, with words,
And save or follow thee. Lo! hearken now:
I bid the gods take back their loathsome gifts:
O spurn them, and I scorn them, and I hate.
Will they prove deaf to this as to my prayers?
With tongue reviling, blasphemous, I curse,
With mouth polluted from deliberate heart.
Dishonored be their names, scorned be their
    priests,

Ruined their altars, mocked their oracles!
It is Admetus, King of Thessaly,
Defaming thus: annihilate him, gods!
So that his queen, who worships you, may live."
He paused as one expectant; but no bolt
From the insulted heavens answered him,
But awful silence followed. Then a hand,
A boyish hand, upon his shoulder fell,
And turning, he beheld his shepherd boy,
Not wrathful, but divinely pitiful,
Who spake in tender, thrilling tones: "The gods
Cannot recall their gifts. Blaspheme them not:
Bow down and worship rather. Shall he curse
Who sees not, and who hears not,—neither knows
Nor understands? Nay, thou shalt bless and pray,—
Pray, for the pure heart purged by prayer, divines
And seeth when the bolder eyes are blind.
Worship and wonder,—these befit a man
At every hour; and mayhap will the gods
Yet work a miracle for knees that bend
And hands that supplicate."
Then all they knew
A sudden sense of awe, and bowed their heads
Beneath the stripling's gaze: Admetus fell,
Crushed by that gentle touch, and cried aloud:
"Pardon and pity! I am hard beset."

There waited at the doorway of the king
One grim and ghastly, shadowy, horrible,
Bearing the likeness of a king himself,
Erect as one who serveth not,—upon
His head a crown, within his fleshless hands
A sceptre,—monstrous, winged, intolerable.
To him a stranger coming 'neath the trees,
Which slid down flakes of light, now on his hair,
Close-curled, now on his bared and brawny chest,
Now on his flexile, vine-like veined limbs,
With iron network of strong muscle thewed,
And godlike brows and proud mouth unrelaxed.

Firm was his step; no superfluity
Of indolent flesh impeded this man's strength.
Slender and supple every perfect limb,
Beautiful with the glory of a man.
No weapons bare he, neither shield: his hands
Folded upon his breast, his movements free
Of all incumbrance. When his mighty strides
Had brought him nigh the waiting one, he paused:
"Whose palace this? and who art thou, grim
        shade?"
"The palace of the King of Thessaly,
And my name is not strange unto thine ears;
For who hath told men that I wait for them,
The one sure thing on earth? Yet all they know,
Unasking and yet answered. I am Death,
The only secret that the gods reveal.
But who are thou who darest question me?"
"Alcides; and that thing I dare not do
Hath found no name. Whom here awaitest thou?"
"Alcestis, Queen of Thessaly,—a queen
Who wooed me as the bridegroom woos the bride,
For her life sacrificed will save her lord
Admetus, as the Fates decreed. I wait
Impatient, eager; and I enter soon,
With darkening wing, invisible, a god,
And kiss her lips, and kiss her throbbing heart,
And then the tenderest hands can do no more
Than close her eyes and wipe her cold, white brow,
Inurn her ashes and strew flowers above."
"This woman is a god, a hero, Death.
In this her sacrifice I see a soul
Luminous, starry: earth can spare her not:
It is not rich enough in purity
To lose this paragon. Save her, O Death!
Thou surely art more gentle than the Fates,
Yet these have spared her lord, and never meant
That she should suffer, and that this their grace,
Beautiful, royal on one side, should turn
Sudden and show a fearful, fatal face."

"Nay, have they not? O fond and foolish man,
Naught comes unlooked for, unforeseen by them.
Doubt when they favor thee, though thou mayest
    laugh
When they have scourged thee with an iron
        scourge.
Behold, their smile is deadlier than their sting,
And every boon of theirs is double-faced.
Yea, I am gentler unto ye than these:
I slay relentless, but when have I mocked
With poisoned gifts, and generous hands that
        smite
Under the flowers? for my name is Truth.
Were this fair queen more fair, more pure, more
        chaste,
I would not spare her for your wildest prayer
Nor her best virtue. Is the earth's mouth full?
Is the grave satisfied? Discrown me then,
For life is lord, and men may mock the gods
With immortality." "I sue no more,
But I command thee spare this woman's life,
Or wrestle with Alcides." "Wrestle with thee,
Thou puny boy!" And Death laughed loud, and
        swelled
To monstrous bulk, fierce-eyed, with outstretched
        wings,
And lightnings round his brow; but grave and firm,
Strong as a tower, Alcides waited him,
And these began to wrestle, and a cloud
Impenetrable fell, and all was dark.

————————————

"Farewell, Admetus and my little son,
Eumelus,—O these clinging baby hands!
Thy loss is bitter, for no chance, no fame,
No wealth of love, can ever compensate
for a dead mother. Thou, O king, fulfill
The double duty: love him with my love,
And make him bold to wrestle, shiver spears,
Noble and manly, Grecian to the bone;

And tell him that his mother spake with gods.
Farewell, farewell! Mine eyes are growing blind:
The darkness gathers. O my heart, my heart!"
No sound made answer save the cries of grief
From all the mourners, and the suppliance
Of strick'n Admetus: "O have mercy, gods!
O gods, have mercy, mercy upon us!"
Then from the dying woman's couch again
Her voice was heard, but with strange sudden
    tones:
"Lo, I awake—the light comes back to me.
What miracle is this?" And thunders shook
The air, and clouds of mighty darkness fell,
And the earth trembled, and weird, horrid sounds
Were heard of rushing wings and fleeing feet,
And groans; and all were silent, dumb with awe,
Saving the king, who paused not in his prayer:
"Have mercy, gods!" and then again, "O gods,
Have mercy!"
Through the open casement poured
Bright floods of sunny light; the air was soft,
Clear, delicate as though a summer storm
Had passed away; and those there standing saw,
Afar upon the plain, Death fleeing thence,
And at the doorway, weary, well-nigh spent,
Alcides, flushed with victory.

bios

CONTRIBUTORS:

Judy Clarence, a retired academic librarian, currently lives with her daughter, grandchildren, three cats and two dogs in the Sierra, California foothills after many years in Berkeley. She plays violin (baroque and modern) in several orchestras and chamber groups, has sung in many classical choruses, and writes poetry constantly. Her work has appeared in Persimmon Tree, Amarillo Bay, Shot Glass Journal, Allegro, and Tigershark, among other publications.

Whitnee Coy, originally from Lexington, Kentucky, was raised by her single mother and grandmother. She now resides in South Dakota with her husband and family, including two kids, a baby, 2 dogs, and a cat. Beyond writing, she enjoys doing stick poke tattoos with her husband. Whitnee holds an MFA in Creative Writing from Eastern Kentucky University's Bluegrass Writers Studio and is deeply involved in education, focusing on equitable strategies like family engagement, Indigenous education, and social-emotional learning. Currently pursuing her Ed.D in Education Policy, Organization, and Leadership with an emphasis in Diversity and Equity, Whitnee has already published two chapbooks of poetry: "Kintsukuroi" (Finishing Line Press) and "Cicurate" (SD State Poetry Society). Her poems have graced the pages of prestigious literary journals such as "Pasque Petals," "Poem Memoir Story PMS," "Jelly Bucket," and "Havik: The Las Positas College Journal of Arts and Literature."

In the past year, **Bailey Grey** has found her flow in poetry. "Hot Girl Bummer" has everything — existentialism, trauma, smut, horrors of working in hospitality as an artist, a letter to her dad, and much more. There's even an interactive element! Bailey is finally ready to release the deepest art she's ever made.

Tamara Holman is a poet, writer, and archaeologist based in Kenai, Alaska. Her poetry has been featured in Alaska Women Speak, Big Wing Review, The Muse, Practicing Anthropology, and elsewhere.

Casey Lawrence (she/they) is a Canadian author and researcher. She published a YA thriller trilogy with JMS Books in 2023 and her poetry and short fiction can also be found in Bi Women Quarterly, The First Line Literary Journal, Polar Borealis: Magazine of Canadian Speculative Fiction, Stone Quarterly: A Literary Arts Journal, and elsewhere.

Barbara A Meier Holtz is a writer living in Lincoln, KS. She loves all things ancient. She works in a second grade classroom and in her free time she likes to drive the dirt roads around Lincoln.

Victoria Minerva was born in Bulgaria and lives there. She is in her middle age and has written poetry since teenage. She loves writing poetry, short stories, and flash fiction. She has two published poetry books on Amazon, and her third poetry book is in the process of publishing.

Suzanne Morris is a novelist with eight published works, and a poet. Her poems have appeared in numerous anthologies and in a variety of online poetry journals including The New Verse News, The Texas Poetry Assignment, Stone Poetry Quarterly, and The Pine Cone Review. Ms. Morris is a native Houstonian, and currently resides in Cherokee County, Texas.

Fiona Richardson is a retired librarian living in Oxford, in the UK. She has a lifelong love of poetry and a particular passion for the poets of the Romantic era, along with their ideals of liberty, equality and a love of the natural world. She tries to bring that Romantic spirit into her own poetry (though hopefully a bit less flowery).

Ellen Romano resumed writing poetry after thirty years when the COVID pandemic and the sudden death of her husband left her with a need to express herself in a new way. She lives in Hayward, California and enjoys frequent visits with her children and grandchildren. She is the winner of Third Wednesday's 2023 Poetry Prize and several awards from the Ina Coolbrith Circle. Her work has appeared in Lascaux Review, Naugatuck River Review, december magazine and other publications.

Holly Payne-Strange's writing has been lauded by USA Today, LA weekly and The New York Times. She has had her poetry published by various groups including Door Is A Jar magazine, Quail Bell, In Parenthesis, and Dipity Lit Magazine, among others. She would like to thank her wife for everything.

Linda Rosewood is a Californian poet who lives in Ireland.

Judith Skillman's poems have appeared in Commonweal, Threepenny Review, Zyzzyva, and other literary journals. She has received awards from Academy of American Poets and Artist Trust. Oscar the Misanthropist won the 2021 Floating Bridge Press Chapbook Award. Her recent collection is Subterranean Address, New & Selected Poems, Deerbrook Editions 2023. Visit www.judithskillman.com

Alexandria Tannenbaum is a poet and National Board Certified educator working outside of Chicago, Illinois. In addition to teaching, she is pursuing a Master of Fine Arts in Poetry. Her poems are published in the magazines Across the Margin, Amphora, Bluepepper, As It Ought To Be, Cerasus, and the book "So It Goes" by the Kurt Vonnegut Museum and Library. Her poems "Elegy for the Loneliest Whale in the World" and "[polite]" will be published in the next issue of Canyon Voices Lit Magazine.

- Substack essays and short fiction
- Of Gods and Globes I
- Of Gods and Globes II
- Of Gods and Globes III
- Bell Hammers: The True Folk Tale of Little Egypt — *historical humor novel*
- Tap & Die — *a "Die Bard" fantasy novella*
- 15 Vale Short Stories — *short stories from the universe where all of his fiction and nonfiction and poetry and photonovels connect*
- The Greenwood Poet — *poetry written during the pandemic in Greenwood cemetery, 500 acres of the oldest rural cemetery in America*
- Inconveniences Rightly Considered — *poems from his twenties*
- Harry Rides the Danger — *children's picture book on courage*
- The Elevator Out — *children's picture book on wonder*
- *H.A.L.T.S. — 90's alt-rock folk album*
- *All Who Wander — indie folk, experimental album*
- *Open — short film written for WRKR productions*
- *Cold Brewed — photo novel (graphic novel with still photographs) in a world where the prohibition made third wave coffee illegal*

Over at http://lanceschaubert.org you can find the archive of 400 academics, artists, and authors published in The Showbear Family Circus, resources for your own creative work, as well as ongoing serialized work by Lancelot.

Thanks for buying, reading, and sharing the work of living authors.

www.ingramcontent.com/pod-product-compliance
Lightning Source LLC
Chambersburg PA
CBHW031753200726
48289CB00013B/868

"A convincing, uncompromising job…"
—*Kirkus Reviews*

"*Cut Me In* by Jack Karney is the story of an unscrupulous cop, and an exciting tale."
—*St Albans Daily Messenger*

"It is a strong novel by an author whose work in a district attorney's office in New York brought him in daily contact with that city's police."
—*The Dayton Daily News*

"The story has an aura of authenticity and an exciting pace."
—*The Philadelphia Inquirer*

"Karney does not hesitate to portray sordid and brutal scenes, but has the maturity to keep them as integral parts of the story — not merely recounted for their own sake. There is good in his people as well as bad; strength as well as weakness."
—*Metropolitan Pasadena Star-News*

"… hits hard and ruthlessly."
—*Wilmington Morning News*